AN ANGEL WITH SINS

RIDDHI GUPTA

Copyright © Riddhi Gupta
All Rights Reserved.

This book has been published with all efforts taken to make the material error-free after the consent of the author. However, the author and the publisher do not assume and hereby disclaim any liability to any party for any loss, damage, or disruption caused by errors or omissions, whether such errors or omissions result from negligence, accident, or any other cause.

While every effort has been made to avoid any mistake or omission, this publication is being sold on the condition and understanding that neither the author nor the publishers or printers would be liable in any manner to any person by reason of any mistake or omission in this publication or for any action taken or omitted to be taken or advice rendered or accepted on the basis of this work. For any defect in printing or binding the publishers will be liable only to replace the defective copy by another copy of this work then available.

TO MY FAMILY

for believing in me and encouraging me always

Contents

Contents

Contents

Preface

Since I was a child I've hesistated in communicating about my feelings and emotions. This book navigates through a series of events I have gone through, and every teen goes through in their lives. This is a collection of poems ranging from dark academia to the blissful serenity of nature. It helps you appreciate the little things in life and hides the desires of millions of young hearts within its pages. Based on the musings of a young girl, it has nothing you would expect from an ordinary fifteen year old, yet everything you need to know about her.

Acknowledgements

I would like to express my gratitude to everyone whose motivation and support has helped me publish my debut book. Firstly, I would like to thank my parents and my entire family who have always encouraged me to work harder and never settle. Many thanks to my best friend who has been by my side from when I first decided to start writing poems to helping me in every aspect of publishing a collection of those poems. I would also like to extend my thanks to all those who have always appreciated my work and helped me become a better poet with their constructive criticism whether in real life or through my online blog. Lastly, I would like to thank all the readers because without you guys this would not have been possible. The best is yet to come!

P.s.

To all my elders and adult members of my family and friends, some of the 'inappropriate' stuff written in this book is purely on the basis of observation from movies, shows and stories and neither I have done, nor it is related to my personal life in any way.

Thank You

My demons have festered

"*If I got rid of my demons, I'd lose my angels.*"

~ *Tennessee Williams*

1. she

She smiles like diamonds
her eyes are of pure gold
and she dances to the songs of the waves,
she plays with stars
her tears drop like pearls
yet her soul,
her soul is made of flames.
She's not your ordinary girl,
might seem like a saint
but damn she's a sinner,
she's a loaded gun, ready to be fired,
you can't beat her
she's a savage,
In being the bad guy
she's always the winner.
Don't get fooled by her beauty
she's an illusion
she's a lie,
she's here to destroy so stay away
there's a devil in her angel eyes.

2. swollen eyes

Striving to attain peace of my mind,
yet unable to do so;
My pessimistic thoughts overshadow me,
my failures
my insecurities
my demons haunt me
they chastise,
I hope someone shields me
from this deadly storm
The storm of my unholy thoughts,
I cry for help,
but people run away,
at the sight of the blood dripping
from my swollen eyes.

3. black hole

broken in so many ways
my eyes are poisonous,
clothes so dark
now they match my soul,
destroying myself a little every day
my heart is damaged
hell is my new home.
even when I close my eyes,
there's nothing I see
but a dark paradise,
everything is blurry
I have a mind of stone,
bleeding in black
trod upon like a corpse,
while the rest of the world seems like a constellation,
I myself am,
just a black hole.

4. underneath

Night and day,
my thoughts haunt me
In my reflection
It's my scars that I see,
As the mirror breaks and pieces fall,
I see the demons
hidden underneath it all...

5. dark monsters

Discovering dark monsters
Lurking within my soul,
I hasten to save myself,
As they follow me from a dimension unknown.
Consummating the pure soul,
They are rapidly ravening,
The monsters that dwelled all along,
Are finally awakening.
A deep dark cave which I was forbidden to enter,
Like a fortress has now opened it's great doors,
With silhouettes and shrieks from each and every corner,
Knowing my survival here is paradoxical,
My face red with terror, my eyes sore.
With fires blazing in my throat
Not the kind you'd like to know,
I try to jolt them down
But they continue to flourish and grow,
The monsters that hid beneath me
Are starting to show!

6. demonic world

I realize
The monsters are not just dwelling inside
This menacing world
is demonic and dangerous,
Refusing to give up
I try to convince myself,
it'll all be fine.
But the world is a marathon with no scope for rest
Even the sky is clustered,
with no space for a single star to shine.
Nowhere for young, innocent hearts to enshroud,
Fighting hard,
alone
Trusting no one,
Since there are plenty of stabbers around.

7. countless sins

Not paying the piper
But the king
Killing a few
along the way,
Tearing apart lives
For a victory of your own
You're the worst demon of all
In every damn way..
Selling your soul to the devil
For just a win
Aren't we all monsters
With countless sins?

8. no way out

I scream, I shout,
But there's no way out,
The dark veiled shadows follow me through,
The deafening silence indicating my doom is near,
My perilous thoughts, killing me too...

9. blood stained teeth

A monster with blood stained teeth
And veins black with poison,
With a pale white face
And eyes of yellow-gold,
She's tragic, she's vicious,
And she's the villain
of all the legends ever told.
Relishing the shivers in your fearful voice
Laughing at your pain and torments,
She feels fulfilled by your agony,
she'd burn you to ashes
Yet you'd still be swayed by her,
She's the purest form of beauty
You'll ever see.
When she walks even the devil's terrified,
She wears her crown with the smile of a saint,
And sits on her throne with utter poise and beauty,
Even the sight of her leaves a mark
She was your past, she's your future,
Even though a nightmare,
She's the purest form of royalty.

10. smiling anyway

losing faith in hope
feeling empty inside,
with my mind all blurred out,
my mental health miserable,
killing me inside
anxiety, depression and what not
sitting in the corner and weeping all day,
even though I'm broken apart on the inside
not divulging my desolations,
and smiling anyway.

11. destroyed

melancholic hearts
unholy eyes
tears on our cheeks
quivering smiles,
used to start our mornings
with laughter
of pain we were devoid
but due to
the sticks and stones of life
with time we were all destroyed....

12. nightmare

I lay drunk in a corner
with cuts on my wrists
wondering if this day is my last,
all my demons have taken over
and with no one there for me
I'm all alone in this fight
I feel like there's a hole in my heart.
As I close my eyes
I'm frightened skin deep,
Horrendous weeps and cries
echoing in my ears
and I see myself walking on paths of thorns,
as I drink lava,
I'm reduced to ashes,
I wake up suddenly
at the sight of the monsters' salient scorns.
I sigh as I realise
this was just a nightmare,
but wait, I'm one too!
I throw the alcohol,
aid my cuts,
Dear angels,
now the devil's tryna be you.

13. a rose with thorns

been trampled for long,
fought all the wars by myself
I let myself bleed
strengthened me, by being sore,
but who was I hiding from?
I myself was my demon,
but no more

no more.
I entered as a rose, delicate and beautiful,
But now I have thorns too,
I am attuned to the pain
so don't tryna quash me now,
because in the end, it'll hurt you!

With brave wings, she flies

"Lift your wings,

And show them how much hell an angel can cause"

~ Wisteria Andrews

14. queen's reign

Like a mirror I shatter, I shatter like shards of glass
but I refuse to quit
even when my body's pale
and blood is dripping from my earlobes,
like a phoenix I rise from the ashes;
I straighten my crown and adjust my robe.
knowing how grievously life knocks us down sometimes,
like a warrior I'll rise and fight again,
I'll be thunderous even if I have a thousand bleeding cuts,
And hence the queen, continues her reign!

15. let's

Let's fight our battles with confidence and conviction,
strengthning ourselves from the pain,
keeping a deadly smile,
let's be fearless and sanguine
in the tragic times.
In the deadliest hours,
with shadowing monsters,
let us be our own guiding light,
our unfathomable dunkirk spirit our sword
our courage, our shield,
Let us be our own field of stars,
when we lose our path at night.
relinquishing every unpleasant memory that brought heartache,
forgetting every argument,
Let us refine our souls,
The golden hour has begun,
in this is a new dawn
we'll definitely see a rainbow,
Let's write a new chapter in our book of destiny
moving forward without looking back,
becoming successful, fulfilling our goals.

16. closely

as each drop of tear
falls off of me,
In my reflection it's my scars that I see
my inabilities and how alone I am
with a shattered and vanquished soul
everything seems a scam.
but as I see my face closely
there's still a slight smile, so pretty,
which gives me a glimmer of hope
for rising back after being knocked down
there is always scope.

17. one shot

we all have disparate journeys,
let's make the most of it,
keep moving forward
even if the pace seems slow,
keep your composure when you're the hardest hit.
spend time with the ones you love,
making enemies ain't beneficial anyway,
and fulfill your dreams
cuz you get only one shot,
party hard, laugh and have no regrets,
apologise to the ones you mortified
Pour your heart out
cuz life's too short!

18. reach in, reach out

when the path seems too arduous to walk through,
and I feel I've reached a dead end,
with nowhere to go,
standing motionless on the pavements,
with no shoulder to lean on,
and feeling utterly alone,
I feel suffocated
I feel helpless;
but after being broken into a thousand pieces,
I finally take a glance inside of me,
a strong, independent girl with a passion for life,
and a self-loving soul
is all that I see.
and then when I reach in so as to activate my powers,
I rise like the sun from the clouds,
so true, it's darkest before the dawn,
I'm someone unique,
different from the crowd!
and now as the jet black road
turns beautiful and pink again,
I seem to think what all the worry was about,
from experience, I would surely recommend,
when the path seems too arduous,
Reach in, reach out.

19. they'll leave

Life's tough
But love makes it tougher,
Be distant,
No one's worthy of you,
You have mountains to climb,
And success to achieve,
Don't let people in,
Sooner or later they'll leave,
and in the process break you too....

20. cheerfully

nothing is stable
life changes every moment,
every second,
you've entered this beautiful world
but why fear to rebel
when you have to die eventually?
the sky is the limit so unshackle yourselves,
It's the little things in life that make it worth living,
so fligh high like a dove
and steer this life cheerfully!

21. it is what it is

Life plays treacherous games
with your heart, mind, and soul,
Picking you up anonymously one day,
And sucking out all of your happinesses, like a black hole.
While some break down
and cry about the problems they ensued,
The others fight back harder
To enhance the day they once rued.
So, whether you lose a friend or fail in a task,
You're allowed to be sad for it,
But sooner or later you gotta rise from the ashes,
Life is uncaring,
It is what it is, deal with it!

22. family

not just our companions,
we must endear everyone around us,
the world indeed is a family,
let's relinquish the hatred that surrounds us.

23. one more mile

break the barriers
demolish the walls,
wreck the obstacles
that are causing your fall.
you are your first priority,
rise up, it's your time to shine,
forget your sorrows,
and add a smile,
success is never too far,
keep moving on,
One more mile,
One more mile!

• 31 •

We're all angels living in heaven

"Heaven is under our feet, as well as over our heads"

- Henry David Thoreau

24. salt on my lips

For me the ocean is more than a dream,
A place where I can find my strayed self,
Framing every moment in my heart
The mere thought of the great blue sea,
Sends a thrilling pulse through me.
And even when I return to the city,
The sun can be seen in my eyes,
The wind in my hair,
The infinite salt on my lips
with the ocean still on my mind,
I've relinquished from all my despairs.

25. snowflakes

a walk with the snowflakes,
a smile on my pale face,
the resonance of whispering shivers,
and the mountains spruced in a white veil.
my heart elates at the sight of
the delicate, untouched and pure
velvet cover of snow's crust,
feeling the chilly air all over my body
like crystals of sugar
I have white lips of snow dust.

26. India

Resembling god's canvas
Where he's painted his greatest creation,
A country with such diverse cultures and languages,
It's an enigma of castes and religions.
In this sacred land of Ramayan and Mahabharat,
The greatest leaders and scientists took birth,
Even the soil here is so pure and divine,
It is indeed a paradise on Earth.
To the world it might be just a country, developing and small,
But to me it's my world, my duty, my India, standing high and tall,
I am ready to sacrifice my life for this country any day,
Fear my country people, it's here to stay!

27. stargazing soul

I lay down on the grass
gasping at the starry night sky,
getting absorbed in contemplating this beauty of nature,
with a slight smile, I give a sigh.
an undying silence surrounds the place
which uplifts me even if the day was tedious,
this breathtaking sight
makes me forget all my problems
and I lose myself
in the darkness so mystic and mysterious.
The fading clouds expedite
perpetual trails of stars,
my eyes sparkle at the sight of
bewitching constellations of every kind,
each telling a story of it's own
and shining brighter than they've ever shined.
from witnessing the glamorous shooting stars
to all my midnight strolls,
the night is truly a wonder to me
I indeed am,
a stargazing soul.

28. sunkissed

The descent of the sun
and the cascading breeze
my heart soars as i witness
the red-orange colours of the sky bleed into the air,
I ornament myself,
sunkissed,
the peaceful aroma
and the chrips of the birds
succour my soul
to relax and repair.

29. i'll come by

perching in a colossal meadow,
gazing at the millions of enchanting, captivating stars in the sky,
surrounded by beautiful flowers of every colour,
looking around,
so as to catch a butterfly.
the serene silence so heavenly,
I feel as if I'm wrapped up in a blanket
that is the mellow warm breeze,
as the nature calms me down
I'm left utterly spellbound,
My eyes shine at the sight of
the moonlight Cascading through the trees.
at the sound of my alarm
I wake up suddenly,
realising all this was just a dream,
a lie,
longing to escape from the shackles of the cities,
Mother Nature, I'll come by!

30. this city

thousands of untold stories being written
the air smells of hope
within the blinding city lights,
It's a city with utmost beauty and poise
a city where dreams come true
a city with umpteen sleepless nights.
a city with endless possibilities
a city with endless oppurtunities
life seems like a movie
so happening, so pretty,
with buildings as tall as a man's aspirations
you're never alone
just on your own,
dreaming
to be young and live in new york city!

31. fallen leaves

the hills flaunting red and gold,
the calm brush of the warm breeze,
underneath the sapphire blue sky,
are the magnificent maple trees.
the gentle caress of autumn season
stealing the sultry summer heat,
precluding the melancholic winters,
peaceful yet filled with 'trick or treats'
like a fallen leaf,
I steer towards the autumn path
and even if I have to tread alone,
the musky sweet smell of the fall leaves
is an unparalleled company,
my heart feels serene
and I never feel as if I've left home.

32. stardust

The yellow drops of stardust
running through my veins,
I'm a star child shackled
by the fervid human chains.
gazing at the stars
and how they shine for me,
with a soul made of flames,
I wish to return home,
yet I feel I am still stuck
in an awful hurricane.
I'm not the only one lost
It's our time to break through
and return to the sky,
with these sparkles in our eyes
and hearts full of trust
and infinite galaxies rippling inside us,
We are golden,
We are pure,
We are stardust!

33. she dreams

she breathes new york
she dreams new york
the beauty of it's golden skyline can be seen in her smile
it's cool wind can be seen frolicing with her curls,
the depth of the hudson can be felt in her eyes
her broken dreams are restored by the city lights
the new yorkers are her family
she's definitely, a new york girl!

34. 'tis jolly season

the air brimming with love and laughter
our faces spruced in glee
amongst the hues of sparkle, shine and glow,
children harmonising to carols,
gratified and with leisure,
with notorious snowball fights and funny snowmen
above the vast conspicuous velvet cover of snow.
our magnificent ambience resembling heaven
where all the quarrels have resolved,
with the beguiling tales
of elves and grinch
the children insomniac,
to catch a glimpse of Santa and Rudolph.
the clinks of glasses and the hurrays and cheers,
a day where families reunite,
the prayers in curches
the blessings of Lord Jesus.
these holiday pleasures dazzle us,
Exuberant for the new year
with new ventures,
Christmas is indeed a very jolly time for us!

35. city lights

holding a bottle of champagne in one hand
my heels in the other,
walking barefoot on the sideway
letting the city lights take me home,
their shine, their sparkle
being reflected by my eyes
they're an unparallelled company
with them around me
I never feel alone.
and as I finally sit on my rooftop
drinking the champagne
I feel my the cool winds gushing past my cheeks,
blood coursing through my veins
I feel calm, serene
to me these lights are spiritual
they give me the peace,
that my soul seeks.
even when I'm at my worst
even when I've given up
they make me feel alive
they make me believe
that even in the darkest times I can be my own guiding light,
and now every time I watch the sun set into twilight
my heart burns

with the burning city lights.

36. all tanned

watching the aqua blue waves
rise and fall,
feeling the subtle ocean breeze,
the calming of the beach
brings my mind at peace,
as I sit under the shade
of the glorious palm leaves.
the musical notes
of sand and water,
the carefree strolls on the soft sand,
and as I walk,
the seashells flip over
I relax in my bikini
all tanned.

A chaotic angel, who fell in love

"Angels descending, bring from above, echoes of mercy, whispers of love"

-Franny J. Crosby

37. just a fifteen year old

I'm just a fifteen year old
I've not the seen world
I've never loved anyone
the way the movies show,
but as of now,
I love my family
I love my friends
and agree with michael scott,
"Bros before hos cuz they always got your back,
when suddenly she's your ho no mo."
I know I'm destined to be with someone.
we all are.
but, we have a long way to go
so my love, please sit there and wait,
I have to accomplish a lot of my goals
I have to become the woman I aspire to be
but you'll always be there in my heart
whenever I write poems,
fantasizing about our first date.

38. bloom for myself

I've always seen
I've always been told
that I'll fall in love
with a handsome boy,
so I searched the world
but I was just trod upon
and in this process
I was the one I destroyed.
I look in a mirror
and that's where I see,
I'm strong
I'm a warrior,
I can be anything I want to be.
There's beauty and poise
in my tangled curls,
eyes like an ocean
with depth and grace,
a smile like diamonds,
unbreakable,
I'm a flower
I bloom for myself
and each petal is a dagger,
This,
this is a queen's face.

After all these years
I finally perceive
my scars are beautiful
and so am I,
I am perfect with my imperfections
I'll be my first priority,
I'll love myself always,
Till the day I die.

39. so wrong

sleeping all day
books are out of sight,
netflix and chill the mantra of life
laughing at Chandler, Peralta and Dwight,
talking to my best friend all day long,
lost in my thoughts, or randomly singing songs,
sitting in my sweatpants and eating all day,
never felt anything to be so right
even though it's so wrong in every way!

40. my guide

With a dazzling smile, contagious to all,
You stand by our sides, when we rise and fall,
You help us achieve our goals and reach the pinnacle of success
You have a heart of gold that most rarely possess.
You foster optimism and confidence in us
With wisdom, style and grace,
While others hold just jacks and queens
You're our guiding light, our ace.
You show us the plethora of opportunities headed our way
Your presence itself is enlightening, you fill our hearts with glee,
You mould us into better versions of ourselves
And shock us out of our complacency
You teach us to broaden our minds, and explore
You're our friend, our guide, our mentor, and the one we fondly adore...

41. fireflies' flame

beneath the luminous stars
dancing amidst the fireflies in June,
lost in each other
laughing and smiling
hearts overflowing with love, so pure.
fingers entangled,
the dazzling eye contacts
everything seems perfect,
life's back on track,
under the glow of the fireflies' flame,
you and me,
our ultimate aim!

42. shattered pieces

A new door, a new world,
A new venture of her life,
A future filled with joy and excitement,
With a sprinkle of hardwork and strife.
She notices him smiling across the room
Intrigued by the depth of his humorous words,
Fascinated, she wishes to be his friend,
And bear witness to the stories of his life, still unheard.
The more they met,
the fonder they grew,
The rush of emotions each time the touched,
Was exciting and new.
But this initial love wasn't permanent,
Snatched from them on a gloomy Wednesday,
But life moves on and so did they,
Assembling the shattered pieces of their broken hearts,
'Right person, wrong time' is what they say......

43. devastated

whenever I felt like I was losing you
I would die a little.
now you've left me dumbstruck and dejected,
and have broken my heart so frail and brittle.
In darkness
you were my light,
happiness
is now out of sight,
you shattered all the promises we made
to stand by each other
in contentment and plight.
I still cherish all the golden memories
which now come rushing back in my dreams,
the heart which would skip a beat when you were around,
Is now entirely filled with yelps and screams.
the sole thought of letting you go
would haunt me night and day,
you meant the world to me
see how devastated I am today!

44. my teacher

You nurture us when we're just tender green plants,
And help us bloom from little buds into brilliant flowers,
You immerse us in your boundless transcendent love,
You teach us to rise from the ashes and access our inner powers.
You bring light, colour, and happiness to all those who encounter you,
And open our minds to show us the wonders of intellect,
You open our eyes to the rainbow of possibilities,
You help us embrace ourselves and introspect.
You're like an angel always looking out for us,
We can feel your love in the gentle breeze,
You've taught us how to make our angel wings flutter,
You're our saviour, the one who always encourages us to seize our dreams!

45. psychopaths

chattering till 2 at night

being there for each other during a fight

our friendship is extraordinary,

pure gold,

laughing at jokes that aren't even funny

and gossiping about everyone,

young and old.

there's no one I'd rather trust,

with my ignominious fantasies,

and my deepest darkest secrets,

no one other than you,

and people think we're psychopaths,

that we are insane,

like Joey and Chandler

we're the best duo ever and we don't care,

we wake up the next day, and do it all again!

from picking out dresses to wear at events,

to being referred to as a couple thousands of times,

and watching, laughing at movies and shows of all kinds,

and sometimes wondering

"What are we? What exactly is life?"

I treasure the memories we've made together,

we don't know what life has in store for us,

we might not travel to our dream destination,

maybe we'll grow apart,
but you're my first love
and you'll stay in the corner of my heart forever,
I'll even smile and shed a few tears if we ever cross paths,
you're my chosen family,
and
I'll be there for you always
remember.

46. hole in my heart

In summer mornings
And winter nights
When I'm alone
Staring at the light
The smoulder on your face
Your calming sight
You're the one I've loved forever
I miss you day and night
I'll let you
Burn me
Kill me
Tear me to shreds
You hurt so much
But it's you
Who I can't
Fathom to forget
There's a hole in my heart
That's swallowing me whole
Wish you'd return
But you're a black hole....

47. bruises of time

from friends to lovers
that's how we grew,
all the songs and dances,
each time we said 'I love you'
I wish I could erase the past,
and stop cherishing the memories we made,
some awful,
some sublime,
now these memories hurt so much,
memories, the bruises of time,
memories, the bruises of time!

48. my shadow

through the catastrophic hours
In my perplexing ventures
you were the one who held my hand,
a ship that shielded me in the deadliest storms,
you're the water I need
when I'm lost
when I lay adrift
In the deadly desert sand.
the one whose applause means the world to me
In my successes
in my triumphs,
your heart is elated, on cloud nine,
In the darkest nights
when I've lost my path,
to guide me through
you're the star that shines.
day and night working tirelessly
your laugh so precious, like argyle,
fighting with herself,
challenging the world,
walking on paths of thorns
just to see her family smile.
your constant motivation leading my path
helping me work with conscientiousness,

In the most strenuous times,
you make me soar
fly high like a phoenix,
you're the rope I hold on to
In my most arduous climbs.
you matter the most
your worth immeasurable,
like a friend,
like a shadow,
you're always there for me,
I'm surrounded by the clouds of dejection and grief,
whenever I see you desolated, unhappy.
the love from your heart
the warmth of your touch
lifts my spirits,
brightens my mood,
with a smile of sunshine and eyes like diamonds,
you're the prettiest
like an angel,
and Yes that's true!
enlightening my soul with good values,
helping me become a better person,
I celebrate my victories, accept my defeats,
with you dear mother,
I wonder if I've ever thanked you
for everything you've done,
for every battle you've fought,
burnt in flames, you're refined,
you are gold, you are precious,

you are like no other!

49. we are unique

There's been a struggle since forever
between the blacks and whites,
Yet I still can't get why the whites are prioritised anyway?
It breaks my heart when I see the innocent blacks suffer,
Why are we still voiceless,
when we hear about their plights everyday?
And now even the asians,
I wonder when we turned into monsters
the evil within us is stregthning day by day.
Our society is utterly racist,
Yes this is a chilling fact indeed,
While the previleged are worshipped for no damn reason
The others are gratuitously beaten till they bleed.
Yes we are stronger when we stand united,
Yet now we've been divided on the basis of our skin colour too,
George, Breonna and the others, I'm sorry,
Because this prevailing racism took your life too.
We need to let go of such racist thoughts,
One's skin colour can't decide the goodness within anyway,
The world is a family
and every life matters,
We need to perceive that everyone is beautiful,
in their own different way!

50. this girl

like a flower in your arms
delicate and gentle
I demand nothing but us,
you and me wrapped up in a blanket
with a heart full of love
full of trust.
the milky way
the bewitching stars
all reminding me of you,
even if we're a light years apart,
this girl, this heart, belongs to you!

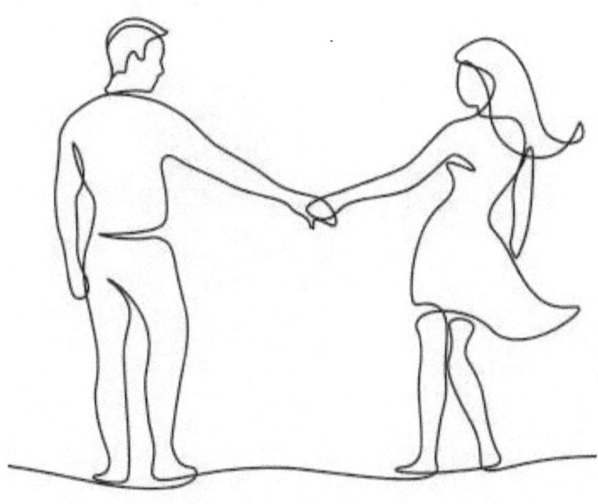

51. the good ol' days

taking a trip down the memory lane
reminiscing the laughs
remembering the wonderful days,
still finding our hoaxes and escapades amusing
as we proceed toward our own separate ways.
contriving delinquent plans we'd renounce at last
playing every known game,
gossiping about everyone we knew
and shamelessly calling out names.
the memories of these delightful times
make my heart smile,
my eyes shine,
we thought that we were friends forever
but maybe that's not how life works
It's time for a final goodbye
and I'll let go steadily, benign.
now we don't even talk anymore
and this is what I condemn,
I wish there was a way to know that you're in the good old days,
before you've actually left them!